I'M ACCEPTED

WALKing the Journey from Rejection to Freedom

WORKBOOK

Holland B. Nance

All rights reserved. Written permission must be secured from the publisher to use or reproduce any part of this book, except for brief quotations in reviews or articles.

Bible versions used in this book are as follows:

Scripture quotations taken from the New American Standard Bible® (NASB), Copyright© 1960, 1962, 1963, 1968, 1971, 1972, 1973, 1975, 1977, 1995 by The Lockman Foundation. Used by permission. www.Lockman.org

Scripture taken from the Holy Bible, NEW INTERNATIONAL VERSION®, NIV® Copyright ©1973, 1978, 1984, 2011 by Biblica, Inc.® Used by permission. All rights reserved worldwide.

Scripture quotations from The Authorized (King James) Version. Rights in the Authorized Version in the United Kingdom are vested in the Crown. Reproduced by permission of the Crown's patentee, Cambridge University Press.

Scripture quotations are taken from the Holy Bible, New Living Translation, copyright ©1996, 2004, 2007, 2013, 2015 by Tyndale House Foundation. Used by permission of Tyndale House Publishers, Inc., Carol Stream, Illinois 60188. All rights reserved.

Scripture quoted by permission. Quotations designated (NET) are from the NET Bible® copyright©1996-2016 by Biblical Studies Press, L.L.C. http://netbi- ble.org All rights reserved.

The American Standard Version (ASV) is rooted in the work that was done with the Revised Version (RV) (a late 19th-century British revision of the King James Version of 1611). This Bible is in the public domain in the United States.

The Revised Version (RV) or English Revised Version (ERV) of the Bible is a late nineteenth-century British revision of the King James Version. This Bible is in the public domain in the United States.

Publisher information

Copyright © 2016 by Holland B. Nance, LLC All rights reserved. Published 2016 Printed in the United States of America

Edited by Adam Colwell
Cover design by Virtual Illustrations Typesetting by Katherine Lloyd

Printing and distribution by IngramSpark

ISBN: 978-0-9982593-0-7

CONTENTS

Introduction 4

Confidentiality Statement 5

Week 1—What Does Rejection Mean to You? 7

Week 2—How Do We Respond to Rejection? 13

Week 3—Willfully Abandon It – Part 1 21

Week 4—Willfully Abandon It – Part 2 29

Week 5—Identify the Lies and Know the Truth – Part 1 35

Week 6—Identify the Lies and Know the Truth – Part 2 43

Week 7—Rejection: the Enemy of Your Purpose 51

Week 8—Be Aware of Devices 61

Week 9—Move from Void to Victory 71

Week 10—TRAIN Yourself to WALK 77

Resources 85

INTRODUCTION

The goal of this workbook is to expand on the teaching and examples provided in the thought-provoking book, *I'm Accepted: WALKing the Journey from Rejection to Freedom*. This workbook serves as a tool to deepen the impact of the information shared in the book to help you advance those thoughts into action and full implementation into your daily life.

You may choose to read the book and complete the workbook by yourself or work in a group of two or more people. Whatever your choice, it is helpful to share with someone that you are engaged in this study so that you can be accountable to that person—so that person can be praying for and with you as you progress.

This workbook segments the four sections of the book into the following ten-week format for the areas of study:

Week 1 – What Does Rejection Mean to You?
Week 2 – How Do We Respond to Rejection?
Week 3 – Willfully Abandon It – Part 1
Week 4 – Willfully Abandon It – Part 2
Week 5 – Identify the Lies and Know the Truth – Part 1
Week 6 – Identify the Lies and Know the Truth – Part 2
Week 7 – Rejection: the Enemy of Your Purpose
Week 8 – Be Aware of Devices
Week 9 – Move from Void to Victory
Week 10 – TRAIN Yourself to WALK

During these weekly studies, you will find Bible study and prayer assignments, exercises, discussion points, and journal pages. Each of these is designed to provide biblical principles, along with practical application to support your journey as you consider some of the most difficult parts of life and make the ever-challenging commitment to WALK in freedom.

CONFIDENTIALLY STATEMENT*

Group Name:_____

Due to the sensitive nature of this study topic, we agree to the following values:

1. **Priority.** Because we believe in the value of community, we agree to give priority to our group meetings. If we are running late, we will call ahead.

2. **Confidentiality.** We agree that whatever is shared here stays here. This includes what is shared through phone calls, e-mails, etc. We want this group to be a safe place to grow.

3. **Participation.** We agree to encourage, support, and stand behind one another, choosing to see ourselves linked together.

4. **Accessibility.** We agree to give one another the right to call in times of need—even in the middle of the night.

5. **Openness.** We will seek to be open and honest with each other. Our small group is a place where we can take off our masks, be ourselves, and be accepted for who we are.

6. **Respect.** We agree to communicate in ways that are respectful, and to give advice caringly only when it is requested. We will strive to be available to one another and listen, encourage, support, and tell the truth in loving ways.

7. **Accountability.** We give permission to group members to hold one another accountable to areas agreed upon.

8. **Open Chair.** We agree to keep an empty chair for others and seek to reach out to people like us who need this place of caring and growth. Eventually we plan to reproduce our group.

Signed: _____

Date: _____

---

* Source: www.smallgroups.com ©2009 Christianity Today Intl

Week 1

What Does Rejection Mean to You?

He was despised and rejected by mankind, a man of suffering, and familiar with pain. Like one from whom people hide their faces he was despised, and we held him in low esteem.

Isaiah 53:3 (NIV)

WEEK 1 – WHAT DOES REJECTION MEAN TO YOU?

Read: Section I – Before the WALK Began Part 1 – My Story

Each of us have had various confrontations with rejection. In Section 1, I share a few of my experiences and how I responded to them.

Read the following Biblical examples. For each, describe the rejection they encountered and list how they responded. For this week, we won't assess the response. We are simply making a list of the responses we observe.

1. Leah: Genesis 29: 16-30:21

---

2. Ahab and Jezebel: I Kings 21: 1-10

WEEK 1 – WHAT DOES REJECTION MEAN TO YOU?

3. Jesus: Luke 4: 16-37

---

4. Now, list a few of your encounters with rejection and describe how you responded.

Week 1 – Discussion Points

1. Take a moment and reflect on your experiences with rejection (no matter how great or small). List them here.

WEEK 1 – WHAT DOES REJECTION MEAN TO YOU?

2. When did the first one of these experiences with rejection happen?

---

3. How has this rejection impacted your life?

---

4. Do you believe this rejection is still impacting your life in any way? How?

WEEK 1 – WHAT DOES REJECTION MEAN TO YOU?

Prayer Assignment

This week, pray about each of the areas of rejection that you have experienced. Ask God to shed light on your responses. There may be some responses that you have not realized before this study.

Journal

Take a moment and jot notes from the Discussion Points and from insights gained through your time in prayer.

Week 2

How do We Respond to Rejection?

He was despised and rejected by mankind, a man of suffering, and familiar with pain. Like one from whom people hide their faces he was despised, and we held him in low esteem.

Isaiah 53:3 (NIV)

WEEK 2 – HOW DO WE RESPOND TO REJECTION?

Read: Section I – Before the WALK Began ·

Part 2 – Where's My Triple A?

Part 3 – Filling the Void to Avoid Feeling the Void

Oftentimes rejection causes us to focus on what we believe we are lacking. Whether that lack is an attribute that we possess or contain within ourselves, like attractiveness, likeability, intelligence, and other capabilities or a lack of material or relational assets. This feeling of insufficiency tends to yield less favorable and unproductive responses.

In first week's Bible study, we reviewed individuals that experienced rejection. One lacked love from her spouse, another received a refusal of an offer to exchange a desired property, and the last lacked support and acceptance from people from His hometown. Leah, Ahab and Jezebel, and Jesus each managed and responded to the rejection differently.

This week we will begin to assess how their responses reflect each person's need for Triple A (Acceptance, Affirmation, and Approval). Describe how each biblical example met their need for Triple A.

1. Leah: Genesis 29: 16-30:21

WEEK 2 – HOW DO WE RESPOND TO REJECTION?

2. Ahab and Jezebel: I Kings 21: 1-10

---

3. Jesus: Luke 4: 16–37

---

4. List the ways you seek Triple A. Are any of these similar to the examples above? How or How not?

5. Do these sources provide temporary or permanent Triple A?

----

6. If temporary, how do you feel when you have to replenish Triple A?

Week 2 – Discussion Points

1. Think of the sources of Triple A. Discuss temporary sources and permanent sources.

WEEK 2 – HOW DO WE RESPOND TO REJECTION?

2. How can you access permanent sources of Triple A?

---

3. Discuss what the term "God-sized" void means.

---

4. In what ways have you tried to fill the "God-sized" void?

WEEK 2 – HOW DO WE RESPOND TO REJECTION?

5. What were the results?

Prayer Assignment:

This week, pray about the results of your responses to rejection and what activities those may have included. Ask for help in determining a Christ-like response when encountering rejection in the future.

Section 1 – Let's Pray

Heavenly Father, I thank you for giving me an opportunity to think about the experiences I have had in my life. I am grateful that you are present with me as I reflect and are constantly protecting my mind. Thank you for the guidance of your Holy Spirit to help me sift through the memories and provide clarity. Please help me uncover any hidden places that are necessary for me to experience the true peace and freedom that you have prepared for me. Thank you for healing my broken places and bandaging my wounds. Thank you for embracing me through this process, knowing that there is nothing that I have done or will do that will cause you to stop loving me. I trust you.

In Jesus' Name. Amen.

WEEK 2 – HOW DO WE RESPOND TO REJECTION?

Journal

Take a moment and jot notes from the Discussion Points and from insights gained through your time in prayer.

Week 3

Willfully Abandon It – Part 1

...that He would grant you, according to the riches of His glory, to be strengthened with might through His spirit in the inner man.
EPHESIANS 3:16 (NASB)

...do not be conformed to this world,
but be transformed by the renewing of your mind, ...
ROMANS 12:2 (NASB)

Brethren, I do not count myself to have apprehended; but one thing I do, forgetting those things which are behind and reaching forward to those things which are ahead.
PHILIPPIANS 3:13 (KJV)

Loose thyself from the bands of thy neck,
o captive daughter of Zion!
ISAIAH 52:2 (KJV)

WEEK 3 — WILLFULLY ABANDON IT — PART 1

Read: Section 2 — Let's Take the WALK Together

    Part 1 — Be WILLFUL

    Part 2 — ABANDON It

In order to shift to a willful mindset, there has to be a decision to become intentionally diligent. This begins with becoming frustrated and no longer willing to tolerate your current conditions of life, knowing that better is available for you. The focus transitions from the pain and fear of the unknown to the potential joy and freedom that awaits.

Read Ephesians 3:16 and describe the phrase "to be strengthened with might through His Spirit."

----

1. Are there areas in your life where you feel "enough is enough"? If so, list them here.

WEEK 3 – WILLFULLY ABANDON IT – PART 1

2. Where should change take place, first? Read Romans 12:2.

---

3. List a few of the ways this transformation and renewal of the mind can take place.

WEEK 3 – WILLFULLY ABANDON IT – PART 1

Exercise: Assess It and Accept It

Use the Chart below to list the aspects and occurrences of your life that have shaped who you are now. Include the positive and negative choices, events, and decisions. I have provided an example as a guide.

Assess It and Accept It (Example)

Event/Issue	Positive or Negative (+/-)	Your Role in this Event/Issue	Statement of Acceptance
Dropped out of college in Senior year.	-	Took too many years trying to figure out what I wanted to study and ran out of money.	I realized that I misused time and wasted money not being focused while in school. I now know the importance of time management and preparation before starting school. I accept my responsibility in this and no longer negatively judge myself for the outcome.
Being sexually abused as a child.	-	I was a child and had little power to fully control the situation.	This is a terrible thing that happened in my life, but it does not define who I am or dictate who I will be. I accept this as a truth in my life and don't consider myself damaged because of it.
Graduated College	+	I went back to school while working full time to complete the degree I started 20 years earlier.	I am grateful for the resilience to complete this goal. It took a significant amount of time to finish, but I am proud that I finished. I accept that I am capable of doing anything I set my mind to.

WEEK 3 – WILLFULLY ABANDON IT – PART 1

Assess It and Accept It Guide

Event/Issue	Positive or Negative (+/-)	Your Role in this Event/Issue	Statement of Acceptance

The power of acceptance is to see things as they are and to stay in relationship with the reality of the occurrences of your life. This allows you to view them in the light of the bigger picture of God's plan of your life as a whole.

Read Romans 8:28 and note your thoughts in this week's journal section.

Week 3 - Discussion Points

1. Share insights gained from completing the Assess It and Accept It Chart.

---

2. Describe how this process felt.

WEEK 3 – WILLFULLY ABANDON IT – PART 1

Prayer Assignment:

This week, pray about the areas in your life that you want to improve. Ask God to strengthen, renew, and reshape your mind and thought process. Continue to ask God to heal and shield your heart from brokenness and bitterness that may want to begin to form as you reflect through some of the more painful times in life.

WEEK 3 — WILLFULLY ABANDON IT — PART 1

Journal

Take a moment and jot notes from the Discussion Points and from insights gained through your time in prayer.

Week 4

Willfully Abandon It – Part 2

...that He would grant you, according to the riches of His glory, to be strengthened with might through His spirit in the inner man.

Ephesians 3:16 (NASB)

...do not be conformed to this world,
but be transformed by the renewing of your mind, ...

Romans 12:2 (NASB)

Brethren, I do not count myself to have apprehended; but one thing I do, forgetting those things which are behind and reaching forward to those things which are ahead.

Philippians 3:13 (KJV)

Loose thyself from the bands of thy neck,
o captive daughter of Zion!

Isaiah 52:2 (KJV)

WEEK 4 – WILLFULLY ABANDON IT – PART 2

Read: Section 2 – Let's Take the WALK Together Part 1 – Be WILLFUL
Part 2 – ABANDON It

Toward the end of the ABANDON It chapter, I discuss the importance of forgiving yourself and forgiving others. We all have a choice. We can hold grudges and allow those grudges to develop into anger, bitterness, or resentment. Rather than attracting healthy relationships, instead, we only pull ourselves toward more depleting and dysfunctional interactions, which lead to further rejection.

Read Matthew 18: 21-35 and describe how this scenario may apply to our experiences with rejection, disappointment and heartbreak.

Exercise: Forgiveness or Suppression

Using the statements below, consider a situation where you have been hurt, offended, disappointed, or rejected and check which ones reflect your current feelings toward that issue.

Suppression-Based Behaviors

Current Thoughts Relating to the Issue	✓ Check all that apply
Forced refusal to think of the issue/person	
Blaming and judging myself	
Talking about the issue to others to influence their thoughts on the issue	
No apology is necessary	
Pushing feelings aside to support the continuation of the relationship	
Decide to not be offended anymore	
Increased pleasure seeking (eating, shopping, sexual activity, working, etc.)	
Risky behavior and thrill seeking to dull the pain relating to this issue	

Forgiveness-Based Behaviors

Current Thoughts Relating to the Issue	✓ Check all that apply
No apology is necessary	
Glad to hear of their success	
Concerned for their well-being	
Pray for God's mercy and healing for them	
Decide to not be offended anymore	
Willing to accept apology, if offered	
Give yourself time to process how you feel	
Reflect on what was learned by the experience	

Each of the responses reflect the state of your heart about the issue. You may even notice that some responses appear on the both lists. You can decide to not be offended from a position of being confident that it is not the person's intention to be disrespectful or you can decide to not be offended from the perspective that the wall around your heart is so impenetrable that no one will ever hurt you again.

Suppression only masks the emotional pain and diverts the focus onto other activities. When an issue is suppressed, it seems to be resolved, but when another occurrence of that or a similar issue happens, all of the original feelings resurface. The key to abandoning the hurtful and disappointing places in life is to take the necessary time to think about and consider the emotions that are generated about these matters. You may choose to use a small group, like this or a counselor to assist you through this process. Once you assessed the thoughts and feelings, commit to releasing it, refuse to live in those emotions, and prepare to evolve your thoughts to those that are empowering and uplifting.

Read Philippians 4:6-8 and write the scripture verses here:

Week 4 - Discussion Points

1. What debilitating thoughts or ideas about yourself and your life are you willing to abandon?

----

2. What are you committed to forgiving about yourself and your life?

Prayer Assignment:

This week, pray about the areas in your life that you seek to forgive. Ask God to strengthen, and empower your thoughts. Read and pray Philippians 4:6-8, personalizing each statement. Continue to ask God to fortify your heart from pain and hurt, while keeping it tender enough to experience His love and those He has appointed to love you.

WEEK 4 – WILLFULLY ABANDON IT – PART 2

Journal

Take a moment and jot notes from the Discussion Points and from insights gained through your time in prayer.

Week 5

Identify the Lies and Know the Truth – Part 1

The heart is more deceitful than all else and
is desperately sick; Who can understand it?
JEREMIAH 17:9 (NASB)

…and you will know the truth,
and the truth will make you free.
JOHN 8:32 (NASB)

To the praise of the glory of his grace,
wherein he hath made us accepted
in the beloved.

EPHESIANS 1:6 (KJV)

WEEK 5 – IDENTIFY THE LIES AND KNOW THE TRUTH – PART 1

Read: Section 2 – Let's Take the WALK Together

　　Part 3 – The Biggest LIE

　　Part 4 – KNOW the Truth

The purpose of every lie is to steer you off the course of finding true freedom. Every lie has the same objective, even those lies that are said to "protect" you. The only way to achieve freedom and the reality God wants us to experience is through truth.

Read and summarize Genesis 2:15-17; Genesis 3:1-5:

In the Garden of Eden, the serpent distorted the instructions God gave to shift Eve's thoughts about God. He wanted Eve to believe that God was withholding something precious from her and caused her to focus on the one thing she couldn't do, rather than enjoy the millions of others things God provide for her enjoyment and enrichment.

WEEK 5 – IDENTIFY THE LIES AND KNOW THE TRUTH – PART 1

Consider this for your own life. What lies have you believed (rather they were based on actual words or information told to you or ideas about a situation that you developed on your own) that have distorted your view of a situation or yourself?

Take a moment and list them here:

How have these lies and the distorted viewpoint impacted your life and relationships?

WEEK 5 – IDENTIFY THE LIES AND KNOW THE TRUTH – PART 1

What is the root of the lies? Where did they begin?

In the book, I describe how I spent time addressing the childhood sexual molestation and pinning this as the cause of the dysfunction in my life. While that was an issue of concern, that was not the core source of the pain and issues I was experiencing. I had to dig deeper.

Week 5 - Discussion Points

1. Now that you have identified the lies and distorted viewpoints that exist in your life, what are you committed to do about them?

WEEK 5 – IDENTIFY THE LIES AND KNOW THE TRUTH – PART 1

2. Which of these issues will you commit to dig deep into and find the core?

---

3. How will you begin this process?

WEEK 5 – IDENTIFY THE LIES AND KNOW THE TRUTH – PART 1

Prayer Assignment:

This week, pray about the lies and distorted views you have been exposed to in life. Ask God to help you forgive those who have lied to you and ask God to forgive you of the lies you have told in response to this distorted view. Read and pray John 10:10. Continue to ask God to provide clarity and insight to the hidden places where the lies may have taken root. Pray for the Spirit of truth to begin to invade all of these places and evict the spirt of deception.

WEEK 5 – IDENTIFY THE LIES AND KNOW THE TRUTH – PART 1

Journal

Take a moment and jot notes from the Discussion Points and from insights gained through your time in prayer.

Week 6

Identify the Lies and Know the Truth – Part 2

The heart is more deceitful than all else and is desperately sick; Who can understand it?
JEREMIAH 17:9 (NASB)

...and you will know the truth,
and the truth will make you free.
JOHN 8:32 (NASB)

To the praise of the glory of his grace,
wherein he hath made us accepted
in the beloved.

EPHESIANS 1:6 (KJV)

WEEK 6 – IDENTIFY THE LIES AND KNOW THE TRUTH – PART 2

Read: Section 2 – Let's Take the WALK Together
    Part 3 – The Biggest LIE
    Part 4 – KNOW the Truth

John 8:32 says, "you will know the truth, and the truth will make you free" (NASB). The whole purpose of truth is to provide freedom. With truth, you have the ability to make clear accurate decisions and view life with a clear lens. Truth provides a stable foundation for life and the pursuit of purpose.

Read Ephesians 6:10-17. Describe the role of truth in these verses.

Why is truth necessary, here?

WEEK 6 – IDENTIFY THE LIES AND KNOW THE TRUTH – PART 2

Truth begins with understanding how God sees us. Take a moment and review the Twelve Things God Wants You to Know list. Read the scripture verses for each.

Twelve Things God Wants You to Know
Review each of these along with the scripture references.

1. Psalm 8 — The Creator of the world cares for you.
2. Eph. 1:4 — Before the foundation of the world, he chose you.
3. Jer. 1:5 — Before you were formed in the womb, God knew you.
4. Deut. 31:8 — God is with you and you don't have to be afraid.
5. Jer. 31:3 — God loves you with an everlasting love.
6. Eph. 2:10 — You are God's hand-made, work of art.
7. James 1:5 — Wisdom belongs to you.
8. Psalm 27 — You don't have to fear anything.
9. Matt. 6:25-33 — You don't have to worry about anything.
10. 1 Chron. 16:11 — God wants to be your source.
11. Eph. 1:6 — God accepts you.
12. Luke 10:27 — God wants you to love Him, too.

WEEK 6 – IDENTIFY THE LIES AND KNOW THE TRUTH – PART 2

There are so many other truths that we should know. Take a moment and write other scriptures that are important for you to know. List them here:

When we are tempted to believe the lies of the past or to fall back into the old ways of thinking, we should follow the example provided by Jesus when He was tempted of the devil. We should state the Word of God and cause our minds to focus and meditate on the truth.

Review the list of lies and distorted views from the previous week. In the space below, write the truth about each of them and find a scripture to support your statement of truth.

Week 6 - Discussion Points

1. Who does God say you are?

   ---

2. How can you KNOW the truth, rather than just recite the truth?

   ---

3. What do you know about God and your worth that you haven't considered before?

WEEK 6 – IDENTIFY THE LIES AND KNOW THE TRUTH – PART 2

4. How can this KNOWing reveal your purpose?

Prayer Assignment:

This week, pray about replacing the lies and distorted views you have been exposed to with truth. Continue to ask God to open your eyes to see yourself as He sees you. Pray for increased insight and discernment to see the truth in others and to begin loving others the way God requires. Pray for the Spirit of truth to be the motivation of every thought and word spoken by you and to you.

Section 2 – Let's Pray

Heavenly Father, I thank you for empowering me to begin to WALK this journey. I invite you and your presence to accompany me as I continue to move forward. Father, help me to be aware that you are here right along with me. You know everything that I am going through as you are peeling away the layers of pain and smoothing out all of my rough places. Thank you for healing me and constantly encouraging me to do more than I ever thought was possible for me.

WEEK 6 – IDENTIFY THE LIES AND KNOW THE TRUTH – PART 2

Thank you for guarding my heart and my mind from depression and suicidal thoughts. I appreciate how much you love me and I am grateful for the gift of salvation. Father, you are all-powerful, all-knowing, and always here with me. I trust you.

In Jesus' Name. Amen.

WEEK 6 – IDENTIFY THE LIES AND KNOW THE TRUTH – PART 2

Journal

Take a moment and jot notes from the Discussion Points and from insights gained through your time in prayer.

Week 7

Rejection: The Enemy of Your Purpose

Today I have given you the choice between life and death, between blessings and curses. now I call on heaven and earth to witness the
choice you make. oh, that you would choose life, so that you and your descendants might live!

DEUTERONOMY 30:19 (NLT)

"that no advantage may be gained over us by Satan: for we are not ignorant of his devices.

2 CORINTHIANS 2:11 (ASV)

For I know what I have planned for you,' says the LORD. 'I have plans to prosper you, not to harm you. I have plans to give you a future filled with hope.

JEREMIAH 29:11 (NET)

WEEK 7 – REJECTION: THE ENEMY OF YOUR PURPOSE

Read: Section 3 – WALK or BEND Part 1 – So Much is at Stake

When we think about the subject of purpose, the life of Joseph provides an excellent picture of a young man who was gifted by God, but encountered rejection, lies, and undue hardship. Joseph paints an amazing sketch of how far off life can seem to go away from purpose, while still being right on course the whole time.

Spend this week reading about Joseph (Genesis 37, 39–45) and answer the following:

1. Describe the rejection Joseph experienced and who rejected him.

---

2. What was Joseph's attitude while he went through the various obstacles?

WEEK 7 – REJECTION: THE ENEMY OF YOUR PURPOSE

3. Describe what might have happened if Joseph became mentally confined by the rejection and hardship he experienced?

   _____
   _____
   _____
   _____
   _____

4. Where was God while Joseph went through the various obstacles?

   _____
   _____
   _____
   _____
   _____

WEEK 7 — REJECTION: THE ENEMY OF YOUR PURPOSE

5. Was Joseph aware of his purpose during all of these obstacles?

---

6. Read Genesis 50:20 and Romans 8:28 and describe how these verses relate to Joseph's life and your life.

WEEK 7 — REJECTION: THE ENEMY OF YOUR PURPOSE

Just like Joseph, all of us have a purpose – reason for living. If you are unclear about what that purpose is, the following chart can assist the process of identifying why you are here and what God wants you to do.

Purpose Guide
The answers to each of these will begin to unveil details of your purpose.

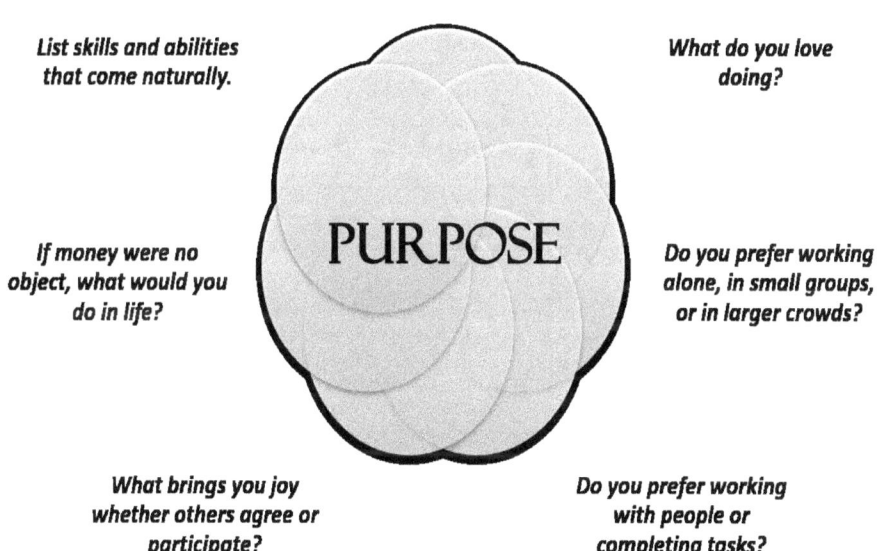

Consider a time in your life when you experienced fulfillment. Describe what that period of time included.

List skills and abilities that come naturally.

What do you love doing?

If money were no object, what would you do in life?

Do you prefer working alone, in small groups, or in larger crowds?

What brings you joy whether others agree or participate?

Do you prefer working with people or completing tasks?

WEEK 7 – REJECTION: THE ENEMY OF YOUR PURPOSE

Write your responses to the statements and questions listed on the Purpose Guide Diagram, in the space below.

WEEK 7 – REJECTION: THE ENEMY OF YOUR PURPOSE

Week 7 - Discussion Points

1. Why is rejection the enemy of your purpose?

---

2. What insights did you gain about your purpose?

---

3. What commitments will you make to pursue purpose more diligently?

WEEK 7 – REJECTION: THE ENEMY OF YOUR PURPOSE

Prayer Assignment:

This week, pray about how your attitude and behavior can impact your purpose. Ask God to grant you grace to endure any current or future hardship or obstacles. Continue to ask God to reveal and confirm your purpose. Pray for opportunities to begin operating in your purpose. Pray for the spirit of humility and meekness as you begin developing confidence in living a purposeful life.

WEEK 7 – REJECTION: THE ENEMY OF YOUR PURPOSE

Journal

Take a moment and jot notes from the Discussion Points and from insights gained through your time in prayer.

Week 8

Be Aware of the Devices

Today I have given you the choice between life and death, between blessings and curses. now I call on heaven and earth to witness the
choice you make. oh, that you would choose life, so that you and your descendants might live!

DEUTERONOMY 30:19 (NLT)

"that no advantage may be gained over us by Satan: for we are not ignorant of his devices.

2 CORINTHIANS 2:11 (ASV)

For I know what I have planned for you,' says the LORD. 'I have plans to prosper you, not to harm you. I have plans to give you a future filled with hope.

JEREMIAH 29:11 (NET)

WEEK 8 – BEWARE OF THE DEVICES

Read: Section 3 – WALK or BEND

    Part 2 – Be Aware of the Devices   Part 3 – Open Book Test

    Part 4 – WALK into Freedom

When we consider the choice we have to WALK or BEND, we must understand that the choice is completely up to us. No longer are we the victim of a duplicitous source that outwits us. We are informed of the devices, now we must make the decision to remain aware.

    Some of the devices come from external sources, but we must also be mindful of the internal devices. The devices that cause self-sabotage, hinder our development, and keep us distant from our purpose.

Read the Book of Jonah (with focus on Chapters 3 and 4).

What were Jonah's internal devices?

WEEK 8 – BEWARE OF THE DEVICES

What were God's responses to Jonah's decision?

How did Jonah's internal devices impact his purpose and his life?

WEEK 8 – BEWARE OF THE DEVICES

Jonah had a few internal devices (hatred, selfishness, disobedience) that God was willing to help Jonah resolve, even to the extent of allowing a few very unusual occurrences. Jonah went through these character building experiences so he could come to the understanding that God loves all people and He desires for all people to hear the message of that love.

Consider your own internal devices. Which character traits in your life are you working to reduce or resolve? The Character Building Guide will help you begin this process.

WEEK 8 – BEWARE OF THE DEVICES

Character Building Guide

Character Trait	Description Details	Results	Counter Response to Eliminate/Reduce	Desired Results
Fear	Pain or threat caused by the expectation of something or someone negative or unpleasant.	Restricted experiences, relationships, and limited life.	Begin to view life from the perspective of expecting good and safe outcomes and being respectfully cautious of dangerous situations.	Fearless, Courageous
Anger	Feelings of annoyance, displeasure, and hostility.	Difficult interpersonal relationships and stress.	Determine to identify the source of the anger and resolve it.	Calm, Even-tempered
Negative-Thinking	Thoughts of unpleasant occurrences and outcomes.	Negative outcomes	Spend time reflecting on positive thoughts, ideas, and memories.	Optimistic, Realistic
Selfishness	Focus mainly on personal benefit without thoughtfulness for others.	Superficial, short-term relationships	Address issues relating to entitlement, pride, and anger. Begin to view and treat others as you would like to be viewed and treated.	Selfless, Thoughtful, Loving of others
Dishonesty	Purposely withholding truth and pertinent details.	Distrusting of others and viewed as untrustworthy.	Commit to communicating only truth and develop willingness to trust others.	Honesty, Integrity
Unproductivity/Apathy	Lack of enthusiasm, concern, or thought.	Stagnant, Inward focus	Reconnect with parts of life that ignite passion and are suitable to your personality traits and skill-sets.	Productive, Caring, Empathy
Over-Compensating	Trying to make up for a flaw, mistake, or issue by performing extreme or excessive tasks.	Feeling underappreciated, stifled, and depleted.	Forgive yourself for past issues, develop love for yourself, and focus on building your strengths.	Confidence, Strong Self-Esteem and Self-Worth

WEEK 8 – BEWARE OF THE DEVICES

Character Building Action Items:

1. I will commit to taking the following actions to build character in
   _____(write in character trait).

   ----

2. I will commit to taking the following actions to build character in
   _____(write in character trait).

   ----

3. I will commit to taking the following actions to build character in
   _____(write in character trait).

Week 8 - Discussion Points

1. Were any of these devices a result or a response to rejection?

   ---

2. In what ways can you determine not to allow these devices to return?

   ---

3. How will you commit to making the choice to WALK instead of BEND?

Prayer Assignment:

This week, pray about the devices that you have encountered through others and those you possess yourself. Ask God to grant you wisdom and discernment so that you are not ignorant when devices are at work. Continue to ask God to reveal and confirm your purpose that no device will delay the process of reaching purpose. Continue to pray for the spirit of humility and meekness as you begin developing confidence in living a purposeful life.

Section 3 – Let's Pray

Heavenly Father, thank you for loving me and accepting me. I ask that you help me fully accept your acceptance. Thank you for setting me free from all of the things that have confined me. I realize that I have allowed myself to remain entrapped by the rejections that I have experienced. Please forgive me for the mistakes I have made and for hurting others as I was trying to find my way. Father, I ask that you guide me as I WALK in your free-dom. Continue to allow my heart to be healed by your Word and allow our relationship to grow closer, through your love. I am grateful that as I continue to WALK closer with you, every broken place in me and in my life is being restored and made whole. Thank you, Father and I love you.

In Jesus' Name. Amen.

WEEK 8 – BEWARE OF THE DEVICES

Journal

Take a moment and jot notes from the Discussion Points and from insights gained through your time in prayer.

Week 9

Move from Void to Victory

Be very careful, then, how you live—not as
unwise but as wise, making the most of every opportunity,
because the days are evil.

Ephesians 5:15-16 (NIV)

WEEK 9 – MOVE FROM VOID TO VICTORY

Read: Section 4 – WALKing in Wisdom Part 1 – How Long Will You Mourn? Part 2 – Moving from Void to Victory

With the information you have gathered from the book, the exercises, and the group discussions, you now have a tool kit equipped with essential pieces to break out of the confinement related to unresolved rejection, heartbreak, and disappointment. Victory comes not only when you begin to master your challenge, but also when you can assist someone else in finding the same freedom you are now living.

As you continue your journey of WALKing to freedom, there will be times when you will have to remind yourself of the process you've started and reflect on how far you've come. You will face future rejection and dis- appointment, but this time you can reach into your tool kit. That is why the journaling is so important. Journaling facilitates the current process, but it also serves as a chronicle to review when you need encouragement and reinforcement.

Read Ephesians 5:15-16 and describe how these verses empower you to WALK to freedom.

WEEK 9 – MOVE FROM VOID TO VICTORY

Are there some rejections and disappointments that can be avoided when you walk in wisdom? How?

What steps will you take when you are confronted with rejection, heartbreak, and disappointment to ensure you do not return to past responses and behaviors?

Who else would you like to see become empowered to manage rejection, heartbreak, and disappointment in a more healthy and productive way?

Week 9 - Discussion Points

1. Which experiences are you committed to no longer mourn about?

---

2. How can you see the victory taking form in your life currently?

---

3. What commitments will you make to sustain the victory you are experiencing?

---

4. How will you help someone else achieve the same victory you are experiencing?

Prayer Assignment:

This week, pray for wisdom. Read and pray James 1:2-8. Continue to ask God to shield and protect your heart as He strengthens you to fully open your heart to His love and provisions. Continue to pray for discernment to identify potential rejections, heartbreak, and disappointments. Seek knowledge and understanding for the appropriate response when these times occur. Ask God to provide an opportunity for you to share the victory you are experiencing with someone else. Spend time listening for God's instruction.

Journal

Take a moment and jot notes from the Discussion Points and from insights gained through your time in prayer.

Week 10

TRAIN Yourself to WALK

Be very careful, then, how you live—not as
unwise but as wise, making the most of every opportunity,
because the days are evil.

Ephesians 5:15-16 (NIV)

WEEK 10 – TRAIN YOURSELF TO WALK

Read: Section 4 – WALKing in Wisdom

Part 3 – TRAIN Yourself to WALK

This week we will focus on TRAINing to WALK. Throughout this group process, we have been exercising the TRAIN method. This week, we will make a few commitments and develop disciplines that will strengthen our ability to WALK.

Use the TRAIN to WALK Disciplines guide to map out the commitments and goals you will set. You can set daily, weekly, month, and annual goals. Make copies and repeat the process as many times as you desire. If you don't reach a goal or meet a commitment, remember every day is a new opportunity. Don't give up on yourself or the process. Always remember, God is faithful. When He sees you are putting forth effort to grow and strengthen your relationship with Him, He will always meet you more than halfway.

WEEK 10 – TRAIN YOURSELF TO WALK

TRAIN to WALK Disciplines (Example)

Disciplines	T – Talk	R - Read	A - Allow	I - Invite	N - Nurture
Example	I will have at least 2 focused times of prayer per day (no multitasking, open conversation)	This week, I will study faith.	This month, I will seek wisdom about career decisions from the Holy Spirit.	Schedule time with Micah and Nicole to discuss their insight on my new idea.	Be mindful of the TV shows I watch and how they affect my emotions.

WEEK 10 – TRAIN YOURSELF TO WALK

TRAIN to WALK Disciplines Guide

Disciplines	T – Talk	R- Read	A-Allow	I-Invite	N-Nurture
Daily					
Weekly					
Monthly					
Annually					

Week 10 - Discussion Points

1. What challenges do you expect to face in carrying out the TRAIN Disciplines?

   ----

2. How do you plan to combat these challenges?

   ----

3. Who can help you be accountable during this process?

WEEK 10 – TRAIN YOURSELF TO WALK

Prayer Assignment:

This week, pray for consistency and diligence. Read and pray Psalm 63:1-8. Continue to ask God to strengthen you to fully open your heart to His love and provisions. Continue to pray for wisdom and discernment. Ask God to bring you people to share your testimonies of His love for you and encourage others. Continue spending time listening for God's instruction.

Section 4 – Let's Pray

Heavenly Father, thank you for caring about every- thing that concerns me. I trust you and know that you are working all of these things together for my good. Father, I ask you to reveal to me the next steps to take as I walk out your plan for my life. Help me to know clearly what decisions to make. I ask that you send positive friendships, mentors, and coaches into my life so that I can continue living in the victory you have given. I need your help in being a good steward over all of the gifts, talents, abilities, and the freedom you have provided. Thank you for healing my heart, more and more each day.
In Jesus' Name. Amen.

WEEK 10 – TRAIN YOURSELF TO WALK

Journal

Take a moment and jot notes from the Discussion Points and from insights gained through your time in prayer.

RESOURCES

Want to know Jesus?
1-888-NEED-HIM

Grace Help Line
1-800-982-8032

National Association of Adult Survivors of Child Abuse
www.naasca.org/

RAINN (Rape, Abuse & Incest National Network)
www.rainn.org
1-800-656-HOPE (4673)

National Christian Counselors Association
1-941-388-6868

Association of Christian Counselors
1-800-526-8673

Crisis Pregnancy Hotline
1-800-67-BABY-6

Post Abortion Counseling
1-800-228-0332

Stop it Now!
1-888-PREVENT

S. A.F.E.
(Self-Abuse Finally Ends)
1-800-DONT-CUT

Suicide Hotline
1-800-273-TALK (8255)

Suicide Prevention Hotline
1-800-827-7571

National Domestic Violence Hotline
1-800-799-SAFE

Battered Women and their Children
1-800=603-HELP

Eating Disorders Awareness and Prevention
1-800-931-2237

Compulsive Gambling Hotline 1-410-332-0402

Focus on the Family (Sexual Addictions)
1-800-A-FAMILY

GriefShare
1-800-395-5755

Grace Help Line
1-800-982-8032

Inform ✻ Inspire ✻ Ignite

For Coaching and Speaking Engagements

Contact:

info@propeltoday.co
www.propeltoday.co

Author – Speaker – Coach –
Creativity Advocate

Holland B. Nance

Coaching and Training to Inspire and Empower Leaders to PROPEL Today in Life and Business

Coming – Spring 2017

Parameters for Productivity:
Moving from Goal Setting to Goal Getting

"Refines the skills necessary to unlock the doors to achieve the goals you set."

Available at:
www.hollandnance.com &
www.propeltoday.co

www.ingramcontent.com/pod-product-compliance
Lightning Source LLC
Chambersburg PA
CBHW050544300426
44113CB00012B/2247